Did You Really Post That On Your Profile!?
Real W.T.F. Dating Profiles

Daniel J Muhlestein

Introduction

A little over a year ago I was in a dating slump. I have
been using Internet dating sites on and off for the past
several years. I have had some success and had some epic
failures too. I enjoyed asking women I would date to tell
me some horror stories about their Internet dating
experiences. I have heard some crazy things in these
stories!

I decided I wanted to see what the Internet dating
experience was like as a woman, so I created a fake female
profile. I shaved my legs, put on a skirt and some stiletto
heels, and had the girl I was dating at the time snap the
photo of the lower half of me for my profile pic.

I used my "female" profile to get a taste of what women go
through every day on Internet dating sites. It was shocking,
hilarious, horrifying, and very educational.

I started a blog where I would highlight different profiles,
both male and female, where it left me just thinking- What
The Hell Is Wrong With These People?? Over the course

of this experiment, I was able to collect dozens of these types of profiles. In the blog I would copy and paste the profile and their photo as they had posted them. I would then add my own commentary below the profile. My words, (blogger commentary) are in all italics.

All identifying information about the people in these profiles I have posted has been removed.

Now sit down, relax, and get ready for lots of Forehead Palming, and exclaiming WTF!!

This Is My First Impression- And This Is As Good As I Get!

About Me:

I'M A [REMOVED] KAT ORIGINALLY , BUT HAVE LIVED IN [REMOVED] FOR GOING ON 17 YRS NOW . I'M A [REMOVED] RAISED KID THAT HAPPENS TO BE BLESSED WITH A TON OF GREAT

FRIENDS AND A GIANT , WONDERFUL , SUPPORTING FAMILY!!! I LOVE BEING CREATIVE LIKE DRAWING , WRITING AND MOSTLY I LOVE GETTING OUTSIDE AND DOING ALL THAT NATURE STUFF AS IN HIKING ,SNOWBOARDING, ANYTHING THAT INVOLVES THE GREAT

DID YOU REALLY POST THAT ON YOUR PROFILE!?

OUTDOORS. I WROTE A BOOK TITLED
, [REMOVED] . THANKS FOR THE LOVE AND
SUPPORT WORLD !! WE ALL BLEED RED SO IN
SOME WAY OR ANOTHER , WE ARE ALL
BROTHERS AND SISTERS OF THIS EARTH AND WE
NEED TO START CARING FOR EACH OTHER AS
HUMAN BEINGS DaS11:18)10.I LOVE ALL MUSIC
AND LOVE HITTING UP SHOWS THE LAST ONE I
WENT TO WAS GWAR , CRADLE OF FILTH ,AND
OZZFEST IN [REMOVED] , I MISS GOING TO
SHOWS , BUT I'VE BEEN REALLY BUSY WORKING
AND WRITING i'm a fun loving , honest and caring guy .
Lifes to short to sweat the small stuff so that's why i live
by an idgaf kinda attitude . I really don't care what people
think about me because I know I'm one sexy beast with a
heart of gold!!

First Date:

HIT UP A STARBUCKS AND TALK TO GET TO
KNOW ONE ANOTHER . PICNIC IN THE PARK . I
REALLY HAVEN'T DATED ANYONE FOR A WHILE
SO WHATEVER IS CLEVER WITH ME , I'M EASY
..BUT NOT THAT EASY ..(;,

Blogger Commentary:

So this guy fancies himself a writer (published a book) I have real doubts about the book given the profile he just wrote. What's with all the shouting in caps? His grammar has something to be desired as well!

So his one and only profile pic is of him just rolling out of bed with his pajama pants on? Wow ladies it can only get better from here!

He may need to ask his mom (whose couch he probably lives on) if it's ok if you come over! lol.

DID YOU REALLY POST THAT ON YOUR PROFILE!?

Looks Like Class- Speaks Like Ass!

About Me:

I always keep it real i don't have time for fake people if your fake keep it pushin. i'm not here looking for a relationship because i already have a man but due to him not being around at this time i still have my needs. i am not interested in bi men sorry but that is just a huge turn off to me, sorry i am not bi never have been and never will be i'm strictly d***y. if you choose to hit me up please keep it 100 because i don't do games, nor am I the type of female that ever chases after a man.

i'm also not interested in anyone younger then 25 or older then 38

if you send me a chat invite and i decline it i declined it for a reason so don't b**ch up and send me a P***y asz email take it for what it is...also if you choose to message me and i say i'm not interested just leave it at that THERE IS NO WHY I AM SIMPLY JUST NOT INTERESTED. If you chose to get at me please come correct bcuz i'm not the type that will tolerate being disrespected. IT IS SO ANNOYING WHEN I GET MESSAGES ASKING ME WHAT I'M LOOKING IFOR LOL IF YOU ARE THE TYPE TO ASK THEN I'M REALLY NOT LOOKING FOR YOU

ps

if u chose to hit me up please come at me better then "whats up" ya gotta atleast give me something to respond to. Also i'm seriously not here for online play..thats just not my style why would i ever want to pretend when i can always have the real thing to me that is a waste of time and fake...and i'm far from fake

LOOK JUS CUZ I'M HERE FOR INTIMATE ENCOUNTER DO NOT COME AT ME SIDEWAYS N DISRESPECTFUL CUZ IF U WANNA COME AT A B*TCH LIKE THAT I GOT NO PROBLEM GOIN TOE TO TOE WIT YO ASZ BELIEVE THAT.

KISSES

Blogger Commentary:

It seems I always find perfect "matches" while doing this blog! The guy below her is looking for exactly the same thing!

DID YOU REALLY POST THAT ON YOUR PROFILE!?

Now I'm wondering, with these girls who are just looking for sex, it seems that most of them have a belief that to be a girl who just wants sex (which is ok- we appreciate her honesty), why do they feel that they gotta come off all gangster scary like? This girl is not bad looking, but her gangster mouth is killing it (the mood that is).

If she spoke like an articulate woman and still just wanted sex, she would probably have much more luck- and higher quality men.

No Skills Here- Just A Hunk of Meat.....
Well If that's What You're Into.....COOL!

Profession: Modeling

Headline: **tall dark sexy model**

About Me:LOOKING TO BE A BOYTOY... i love art. i do some modeling sometimes too but not really into it. I am very busy with my studies and not looking for anything serious right now. i am just looking 4 a nice girl who doesn't mind meeting up on occasion to have some long,

DID YOU REALLY POST THAT ON YOUR PROFILE!?

hot, hard sex! I do have a picture--can email it to you if interested

First Date:

chat a bit, then off of to the jungle

Blogger Commentary:

Ahhh another guy who as found his only real value to society! He must have realized that since he's probably dumb as hell, which is why he didn't even bother photographing his face. He is just going to exploit his only asset (for now) which is his body.

Ladies, he seems somewhat self-absorbed. If you do get with this guy, be prepared for a selfish douche bag at least. Also be prepared for someone who lacks skill. What you'll get is a Neanderthal hunk of meat that does all but bring his caveman club to bed!

Look At Me! I'm About To Become A Statistic!

Headline: **They call me BigBooty for a reason**

About Me:

1.) My hobbies include walking on the beach, dancing on tables at parties, sleeping naked, reading 50 shades of grey, hanging out with my friends.
2.) I am definitely loud and confident at everything I do.....especially in the sheets ;)
3.) I love gospel music.
4.) I love statistics
5.) I love caterpillars
6.) I take a shot once a day.
7. Hope you can handle me :)

DID YOU REALLY POST THAT ON YOUR PROFILE!

Blogger Commentary:

......Now I know that some girls like to listen to music while having sex, I wonder if while she's being confident in the sheets, that she likes to listen to gospel music at the same time?

She loves statistics too- this is good, because there are plenty statistics on young girls who behave irresponsibly- to wit:

Date rape
Pregnancy
STD's
Arrest
DUI

At least she is somewhat literate- what with reading 50 Shades of Grey and all. She likes to keep fit by walking on the beach (probably because all her friends left her face-down drunk, and she walks home frequently). Dancing on the table (I guess that's exercise too).

Adonis Tiger Blood Drinkin' Man Seeks Female Worshiper

DID YOU REALLY POST THAT ON YOUR PROFILE!?

Headline: **This nice guy does not finish last**

About Me:

Thanks for looking at my profile I wonder if you hate reading these as much as I do typing this out.

A little about me a white 31 year old prof male that just completed my MBA so I am looking to let some steam off.

My stats are 6'2", 215lbs, w an athletic build and very fit. I work out 5-6 days a week and eat healthy but I do like to have my fun too, sometimes I admit it does get the better of me. I am a huge sports fan, yes Eagles, Phillies, and

Flyers dont have to be a sports fan but it would be nice to have that in common.

Adventure is a big part of my life so if you like motorcycles, amusement parks, sky diving, and bungee jumping we should talk. Pretty much open minded and willing to give anything a try.

Guess what makes me different is what you see is what you get I dont hide who I am nor should you. I am genuine, honest, sincere but dont let that fool you I know what I want and get it. Not the type that like to sit on his ass saying what he wants to do and never does.

So if you read this far feel free to say hi, I promise I wont bite, unless you want me too (Oh yeah I am a little sarcastic sometimes.)'

PS. I had a stalker on another site and it was full of drama. So I am little hesitant about putting other pics up but do have them in private.

First Date:

I do like the conventional dinner and movie date but not for a first. I like fun, I am speed freak, so first date would have to be an amusement park (I love roller coasters), the zoo, white water rafting, rock climbing just something out of the box and different.

DID YOU REALLY POST THAT ON YOUR PROFILE!?

Blogger Commentary:

This guy reminds me of Charlie Sheen- WINNING!! It's good that guys have high levels of testosterone - it's what separates the men from the boy's right? This guy seriously needs to dial it down a bit.

I'm glad that he specified in his profile that he is a white male- because that's not obvious in looking at his photos (well not counting the blurred photo- what the hell is that about anyway?!)

It's interesting how all of his photos are "self-portraits" ......What's-a-matter muscle boy, nobody can stand to be around you long enough to take your photo?

Women, to hang with this guy, you just may need to pop a couple shots of testosterone yourself to match the megalomania oozing from this guy.

Circus Freak- Sideshow Sally

Stats:

Profession: Snake oil salesman

About Me:

I'm fueled by curiosity and a lack of impulse control. I'm a hot mess. I don't know if my life is meant to be one big surprise adventure after another or if maybe one day I'll settle down. I like to feel special and needed. I think I'm smart and well rounded and interesting. I'm not drowning, but I'm sure as hell not saved. I can be abrasive and tactless at times, but I'm a sweetheart and don't mean any harm.

Books: I like to read neurology textbooks. Charles Bukowski makes me feel pretty. Henry Miller makes me want to write. The Phantom Tollbooth always makes me

DID YOU REALLY POST THAT ON YOUR PROFILE!?

smile. Sometimes I read biographies. Louis L'Amour makes me wish I was a pioneer. H.L. Mencken's written volumes on the American language and I love reading them. I'm always interested in reading something new... recommendations anyone?

Music: I've been told I have poor quality control so I won't go into specifics.

Movies: I like having Spaghetti Western marathons. I like watching movies about the circus and sideshows. Italian horror is beautiful and grotesque and I love it. I love the classics... black & white and technicolor. W.C. Fields cracks me up. Katherine Hepburn's laugh is amazing. Musicals starring Danny Kaye fill me with joy. Werner Herzog is my favorite director. A few other favorite directors are: David Cronenberg, Harmony Korine, Jan Svankmajer, Alejandro Jodorowsky, John Waters, Herschell Gordon Lewis, Mario Van Peebles, Sergio Leone...

Blogger Commentary:

Well perhaps I have found a match for the freak below this post! No face tats on this girl and for that we thank you! But she seems just as weird!

Look What The Devil Spawned! -Run Away!!

Stats:

Education: High School

Profession: Construction

No Children

Headline: **Why do Humans make me hide?????????**

DID YOU REALLY POST THAT ON YOUR PROFILE!?

About Me:

I love books more than I like most people and even love the smell of a new book.

I hope one day to have my own personal library where I can lock myself up in for days at a time.

I love an intelligent conversation and without this there can be nothing further.

What else can I write but that I'm a very sarcastic person and i have a dry sense of humor.

and I'm the Devil

and also a priest with all honesty

Shall I elaborate further, well I'm kinder than most, I care more than most, and I do more than most! I am personally at the point where I should never trust a single person ever and all I really wanted is little and insignificant just honesty and trust which is so hard to come by these days! But by all means prove me wrong I'm waiting for someone with intelligence and while your at it pick up your pitchforks and torches and kill the monster

I love the sound of a piano and the sound of the ocean, I like to travel with nothing but my own two feet and I love to help people even when it's not in my best interest

Blogger Commentary:

Now I've never been one to conform to "social norms" but REALLY DUDE? This guy may have the perception that HE is the "normal" one and that the rest of us are the abnormal, he can think what he wants to think, but he better not be all shocked and shaken and feeling "misunderstood" when society as a whole flatly shuns him.

There may be a girl just as fringe as him (just check this blog), and for the sake of all of us, I seriously hope he finds her.

DID YOU REALLY POST THAT ON YOUR PROFILE!?

...As I Gaze Down The Valley Of......Oh Wait....Nevermind!!

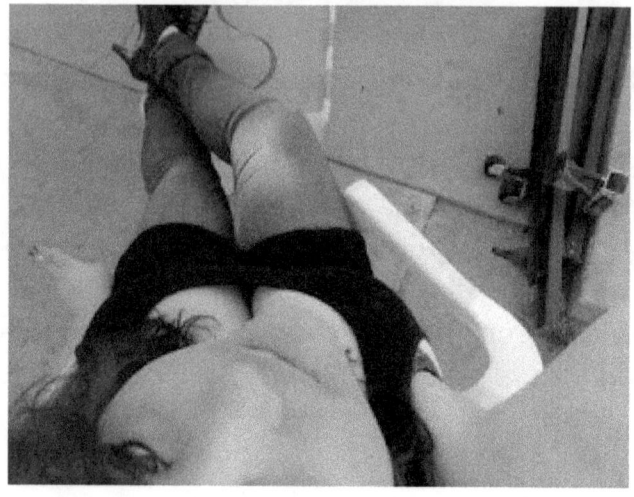

Blogger Commentary:

I just gotta say, this is one of the more "interesting" camera angles I have seen in a long time!

Dude Looks like a Lady-
And Other Observations

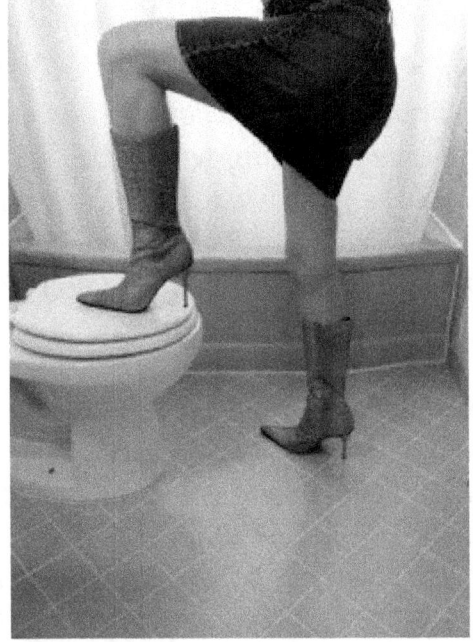

Blogger Commentary:

Last night I logged onto the dating site as my "female" profile. I posted my "legs" photo and again my inbox blew up! I decided to have some fun with it.

I chatted with a bunch of the guys for several hours. The following are a few comments and observations I would like to make:

DID YOU REALLY POST THAT ON YOUR PROFILE!?

Most men are illiterate, knuckle-dragging Neanderthals! They can't formulate a sentence to save their lives. They obviously haven't heard of the theory that if you want people to be interested in you, you first need to be genuinely interested in them. The men I encountered last night were interested in seeing what THE REST OF ME looks like, They were interested in video chatting, texting me, calling me- all presumably to get me in a position to where they can be inappropriate. I had no part of that [obviously].

I let the men know that the reason I don't have a photo of my face online is because of "all the bad experiences I have had" [lie]. I further let them know that it is obvious that I am not overweight and that I am in great condition [refer to legs photo] and that I want someone to get to know ME as a person, not distracted by what I look like.

I called multiple men out on the "lines" they were trying to feed me. One that stands out is this guy messages me and says that he wants me to text him a photo of me and that he PROMISES that he will delete my phone number. LMAO Whatever! IDIOTS!!

One of the realizations I'm beginning to see is that single men and women both want very similar things. They all want love, affection, and intimacy. And in the online world, "packaging and presentation" is EVERYTHING! You cannot come up to a woman online (or anywhere for that matter) with the attitude of they OWE you a picture or

24

anything. Nobody OWES you ANYTHING! You cannot think that you are THAT good that you can just come out and ask for sex talk, photos, or anything like that right away. The "ASK AND YE SHALL RECEIVE" mantra is void in this instance.

After having posed as a woman online and experienced briefly what women experience daily in the online world, I have so much more respect and empathy for them and what they have to put up with. I just hope that these lessons will stay with me and that I will never come off to a woman the way that these men have in this experiment.

DID YOU REALLY POST THAT ON YOUR PROFILE!?

This Is How The Hoochie Mamma Checks Your Oil!

Headline: **Looking for a hard working romantic man**

Profession: security officer

About Me:

Me and my man

First Date:

Full of romance ...

Blogger Commentary:

Here we have a girl just praying to the gods that some dumb rich guy will scoop her up. Because good looks is all she has! We all know what happens to those looks- time will not be kind to her I'm sure!

Says she is a security guard. For what? Victoria's Secret?

DID YOU REALLY POST THAT ON YOUR PROFILE!?

Look What Ronald Found
On The Dollar Menu!

Profession: collage for Massage

About Me:

i have 2 great kids 1 19 girl an a boy 13.. they live for ther mom... 2 dogs,

Im going to school for massage....

i like to shoot guns at targets down field like 100 yards or more.

i like to cook.

dont watch to much T.v

if you wood like to no more just ask.....

WHY IS IT THAT MOST OF THE WOMEN ON HERE
JUDGE A BOOK BY THE COVER AN NOT THE
STORY INSIDE.......

First Date:

some where we can talk an get to know each other over a
drink or dinner what ever as long as its fun....

Blogger Commentary:

*Well to answer your question about why women judge a
book by the cover is because you are posing with Ronald
McDonald, looking like a slouch, and can't spell correctly
(including the word "college"). All of that does not lend to
gaining any kind of instant credibility (which is what your*

DID YOU REALLY POST THAT ON YOUR PROFILE!?

profile should inspire). What this profile screams is, I'm too lazy to put a flattering photo of me on the profile, and I don't pay attention to details, among other non-attractive traits.

How Come Cougars In The Movies Are Way Hotter Than These?

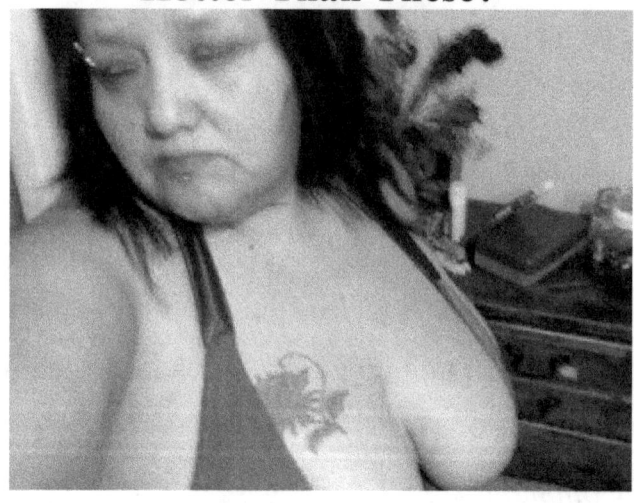

Profession: Cougar

About Me:

WOW IM ONE DOWN TO EARTH COUGAR I LIKE MAKEING FRIENDS N I AWAYS SAY SMILE N THE

WORLD WIL SMILE BACK I HAVE RESPECT
HONESTY N TRUST N IF U CAN HANG WITH THIS

THAN WE R GOOD TO GO..ASK ME ANYTHING I
JUST TELL!!!

First Date:

MY FIRST DAT IS ALWAYS A MYSTERY COZ U
MAY NEVER KNOW WHO'S REAL N WHO'S NOT
LOL

Blogger Commentary:

*I always love an honest woman! I wonder why she is
concerned about "WHOSE REAL N WHO'S NOT?" If both
of you are DTF, then what's the problem? It doesn't seem
as though she wants a relationship or to take someone to
Sunday dinner here! LOL.*

DID YOU REALLY POST THAT ON YOUR PROFILE!?

Ahhhh the Power of Positive Thinking.......
DIDN'T WORK FOR THIS GUY!

About Me:

i have been a mess i am an ***hole and i am a ****ed up
guy i guess maybe i beat myself up to much but i have to
do something i have to change something

First Date:

Anything.

Blogger Commentary:

Weather forecast: Black clouds, rain showers, depressing as hell! Perhaps for his first date he may want to just get all hard core and snort lines of Prozac! It probably will do him some good. I wonder if he is looking for someone just as morose as himself. This guy is depressing me just looking at him!

I'm Bettin' All My Cards That My Temporary Cute-Ness Will Carry Me The Rest Of My Life. Cuz I'm Dumb as Fuuuuuu....

About Me:

hi guys im [REMOVED] ima thinking im not gona b on this one for long so who knows..i love too hang out with my friends and family..n im just looking fa that right guy i meane i know he is out there for me im just not looking hard tho..message me if u wana no more...............bored AF AHHHHHHHHHHHHHHHHHHHHHHHHHHHHHHHHH HHHHHHHHHHHHHHHHHHHHHHHHHHHHHHHHHH

HHHHHHHHHHHHHHHHHHHHHHHHHHHHHHHHHH
HHHH HELP...ok men i love the colors blue n pink they r
my fav colors and i love pizza and freach fries i mean i
love freach fries n chcoclate...

what i look for n a guy is

1.he has too sweet n smart
2.i like a guy that knows what he wants out of life
3. blue or brown eyes i like my men tall
4.must have a good job
5 must no how too treat a lady..
well thats it fo no guys hit me up if u wana get too no me i
mean i like fun....and one mo other thang i love Country
muisc and rap.my fav is hunter hayes,carrie
underwood,brentley gilbert....well thats it for now ill add
mo later

Blogger Commentary:

*You know it's a shame that beautiful girls like this become
so vile and ugly the second they either speak or attempt to
type a sentence! Someone needs to seriously tip them off
that only the broke-ass-gangstas think they are cute. Note:
She mentioned that her guy must have a good job.
Presenting herself in the way she does will only attract the
broke-ass douche bags who don't know how to treat a lady.*

DID YOU REALLY POST THAT ON YOUR PROFILE!?

Besides, I'm pretty sure even SHE doesn't know what it's like to ACT like a lady- forget being treated like one!

The spelling and grammar issues in her post? I've beat that dead horse ad nauseam in this blog!

Daniel J Muhlestein

Hey Cinderella, I Got Your Lost Slipper Here! I Hope It's A 10 1/2!!

DID YOU REALLY POST THAT ON YOUR PROFILE!?

Profession: **Nissan,footlocker, metro parks**

About Me:

I'm very silly always having and lookin for a good tim$e u will always hav a good time wit me I have 3 jobs an a full time student an also teach swim lessons an water aerobic class so in very busy so when I'm free I hav to hav fun an be in stress free environment jus lookin for a good time all expenses on me get at yo boy if u lookin for a good time

Blogger Commentary:

First of all, you gotta love that his main profile pic is on a bike that he obviously couldn't afford, which is why he is posed in a motorcycle dealership! WTF! Let's go to a Ferrari dealership to snap a photo of me sitting in a car I'll never own! Who does this! HONESTLY? - Oh yeah, the same guy that overextends his Footlocker employee discount!

Well if you're into guys who pose on motorcycles they can't afford, horde Footlocker shoes, has horrible grammar, and guides you to their Instagram page [NOT LISTED], this is your boy! You're gonna love him - for like 30 seconds- and then you'll want to RUN!

DID YOU REALLY POST THAT ON YOUR PROFILE!?

Ridden Way Too Hard Last Night- But Just Snap The Damn Photo!

Headline: **WANT TO MEET UP TONIGHT**

About Me:

WHAT UP??LOOKING FOR INTERESTING NIGHT.LETS MEET OVER DINNER AND SEE IF YOU CAN FILL SOME DESIRES I HAVE,SATISFY NEEDS YOU HAVE AND HAVE A GOOD TIME TOGETHER,NOT LOOKING TO BE IN RELATIONSHIP AT THIS TIME.IM IN TO THINGS IM SURE YOU WOULD REALLY ENJOY ,MEN ONLY THOUGH-looking for real deal,no players, I AM REAL AND I DONT LIKE TO SET DATES AND NO SHOWS.I DONT DRIVE SO YOU WILL HAVE TO.IF YOU LIVE OUTSIDE [],DONT TALK TO ME UNLESS YOU ARE GOING TO MEET ME, IM NOT

ON HERE FOR CHAT BUDDIES.WILL EXCHANGE
PHONE NUMBERS.HOPE TO HEAR BACK.-------lol i
just made a funny-POF IS TOO MUCH CLICKING NOT
ENOUGH****NG

First Date:

DINNER,TALK TAKE FROM THERE.BUT IT HAS TO
BE IN PUBLIC PLACE TO BEGAN WITH.

Blogger Commentary:

*She's honest and she love to shout (IN ALL CAPS). I would
venture to guess that's the way she is in bed too?*

*My question to women like this (because this is the second
one recently on this blog) is why is that it seems that you
had your latest conquest snap your current profile photo?
You're all haggard and worn out- what a better time for a
photo! lol*

DID YOU REALLY POST THAT ON YOUR PROFILE!?

He Just Got A "D" In College And Class Hasn't Begun!

About Me:

I am going back to colledge to make the rest of my life easier. Love kids and don't mind watching them once in a while.Get along with everyone,have no enemys. Think life should be fun not stressful. Take it as it comes kind of guy.

First Date:

Whatever she wants! I'm not picky.

Blogger Commentary:

1992 called and Chuck Norris wants his look back! I really hope he pays attention in college this time around, because he already has a"D" in the subject! He really does seem like a great guy- just really has no clue! I'm thinking he really does need to be a little pickier about quite a few things, including his first dates.

Pneumatic Mammories with a Side of Cornhole (The Lawn Game You Sickos!!)

Stats: Non-smoker with undisclosed body type
Interests:
Shoes
Football
Fishing
Shopping
Tattoos
Golf
Rugby
Hunting
Beach

Beerpong
Baseball
Basketball
Mudding
Moonshine

Cornhole

About Me:

ROLLLLLLLLLLLLLLLLLLLLLLLLL TIDE

Born and raised in [REMOVED],, in [REMOVED] going to the golf academy until the end of August..

looking to meet some cool new people...

First Date:

........surprise me

DID YOU REALLY POST THAT ON YOUR PROFILE!?

Blogger Commentary:

By this point in the blog, we are not surprised that here, again, we have another buxom beauty milking the camera time and screen time for her voluptuous assets. Her eyes are barely visible in the shadow of the twin peaks.

Jesus Freak Is....Well.....JUST A FREAK!

About Me:

The key to any success begins with our Heavenly Father and His Holy Son Jesus Christ, honesty and truth.

I was born and raised in [REMOVED]. After high school, I joined the Army and completed three combat tours. I decided to get out and pursue a college education, in which I graduated with my Master's. I love to learn. I enjoy anything that can challenge me intellectually; however, that doesn't mean drama or playing silly-little mind games. Be true to yourself, and anyone you invite into your life. I also enjoy the performing arts, romanticism and history. I

DID YOU REALLY POST THAT ON YOUR PROFILE!?

believe intelligence is a natural aphrodisiac, in all sense of the word. I would like to meet someone that has common interests, is intelligent, believes in God, family-oriented, believes in communication and is in tune with her self and surroundings. I would like to meet and make new friends and go from there. I love to laugh and make people laugh, so a sense of humor is a must. I know we all have had bad experiences in the past, but don't judge me from your past experiences, I won't. Honesty is a huge plus with me.

This may sound like I'm jaded but I'm really not. <u>I have a sense of humor and I do try and find humor in situations.</u>

Sorry to emphasize this; however, please make sure that the pictures you have posted are rather recent and not older than 6 months. Sorry, there's a story there.

If you are currently married and, here's the kicker:

don't want to be; and/or,

think that the two of you may separate; and/or,

he is not home enough; and/or,

he won't watch Friends/Mad About You/Golden Girls with you twice a day or crime episodes all day; and/or,

think that he doesn't love you anymore; and/or,

tired of being married; and/or,

just looking for some thing on the side; and/or,

or whatever sorry excuse you may conjure up, DO NOT RESPOND PLEASE! I am not into that; not now, not ever.

I do try to make light of some women that I have encountered. One more rant and I'm done. Please pay attention to this part, it's also very important. Please, please, please don't ever ever ever e-mail me if:

-You can't read this ON YOUR OWN, or don't understand my profile.

-You don't know where you live (what city).

-You have more facial/chest/back or for that matter, body hair, than men.

-If your idea of a fun-filled night includes checking in every place we go, on your phone, so you can be the "mayor" of that place.

-You have to have an alcoholic drink on a daily basis or your idea of a good time must involve alcohol.

-If the words in your profile are merely a quote from someone not yourself.

DID YOU REALLY POST THAT ON YOUR PROFILE!?

-The only few pictures you "happen to have" of yourself are older than 6-7 months because you "are always the one taking pictures and find it hard to take one of" yourself.

-Fi yuo cnt spel like i kan.

-If you feel the need to e-mail me and criticize my profile, tell me how jaded I am, blah blah blah, you are definitely one of the weird and psychotic women that I am making reference about. If this offends you, :)

-You just started telling your parents 6 months ago that you love them because you are not "an emotional person."

-Think it might be fun for me to join in a sexual encounter with your husband/boyfriend and you or have them watch you and I have sex.

-"Hey" "Hello" ";)" and/or "loved ur profile" are the only things you put in the body of an e-mail sent to me.

-When we actually do start communicating, you suck every second of the conversation to talk about you, what your ex did to you, how you know everything, blah blah blah.

-You feel that the entire universe, to include God, should be at your summons.

-For some psychotic reason, those pictures taken of you 5 years ago, you know the ones where you are 5 years younger than you are now, are your posted pictures.

-The pictures that you do have posted are more of a progressive time line, beginning about 20 years ago and updated one picture for every 2-7 years.

-Think that plasma TV's has something to do with human blood.

-You judge things that you and your date will do based on what your ex did to you; or can't just get over the fact that he left you, or you him.

-For some strange and weird reason my profile offends you.

-If As The World Turns, Guiding Light, and Days of Our Lives get their plot ideas from your life.

-You speak/write in texting lingo, a lot. If so, AMF U SCB (I had to actually look these up to make this up).

-You have to ask me things that are already in my profile such as where I was born because you won't take the time to read, or can't read. If that's the case, you aren't understanding what I'm saying about you anyway.

DID YOU REALLY POST THAT ON YOUR PROFILE!?

-The pictures(s) that you do have posted are of possibly you and several of your female friends together in each picture, some of whom can fit the characteristics described in age, ethnicity and body type. In other words, I have to play "Guess which one I am!"

-If your precious dog Foo Foo has more real teeth than you do.

-You are considering running for the president of man-haters club, or currently serve in an official or ex-officio position.

-The only picture posted is one of an animal or nature or menu or ...

-You have more than one personality, been told you do by several people to include mental health official(s), or recognize it yourself, and then try to blame it on your astrological sign.

-You have more pictures of your feet and toes, than you do of yourself (aka your body). Or heck, for that matter, any pictures of just your feet and/or toes posted on your profile. What's up with that? That's just weird.

-Finally, at the height of your sense of fun, you feel that showing me your butterfly collection will somehow, and miraculously, woo me over, hmmmmmmmm.

If you believe in God, and I hope you do, then you accept Jesus Christ as His Holy Son and our Savior. This is a must (non-negotiable, do not understand those that don't believe). I try to live for Him. I don't go to church like I should but my Faith is solid.

Blogger Commentary:

I actually kinda liked this guy's profile- It's an effing novel, but I found his list at the end to be humorous. The Born-Again-Christian plugs at the beginning at the end were a bit much. I have nothing against his faith; I just think it's best to keep Jesus out of my profile. (I'll keep Him in my private life).

DID YOU REALLY POST THAT ON YOUR PROFILE!?

Just Another High-Paid Fire Pole Maintenance Girl!

Headline: **keep it 100 or fuk off**

Profession: Self Employed

About Me:

Since y'all think I left this paart empty I'll put sumtin first off if I don't reply to ur message it cuz I have no interest so don't send it 109 more times its not. Going to happen lmao don't try to come at me with dat pimp talk u want to recruit go to the stripclub and if u old enough to b my grandfather or father bounce I ain't wit using viagra oh n those here for intimate encounter or dtf don't bother I'm not a hoe and u won't get none lmao ok that it for now since y'all were complaining bout it being empty

Blogger Commentary:

Self-employed in a part of the country where people pay top-dollar for tight bodies. I'm sure that she is just a well-paid fire pole maintenance girl.

DID YOU REALLY POST THAT ON YOUR PROFILE!?

Snap-Back Sitin' Like A Bottle Cap!

About Me:

wat im look 4 in a woman is sumbody tat nice tat got sumthing going 4 them self sumbody tat fun to be around who is funny nt all tat serious n i also want a gurl tat i can be there bestie n there boyfriend im 19 i lyke to hang wit friends party i work i go to college try to learn criminal justice maybe one day be a police officer n move up to crime scene investigator music i lyke is rap and hip hop artist are Tyler the creator lil Wayne Tupac biggie Eminem n drake at time

Blogger Commentary:

You gotta love it when you can hear this person's Haitian accent just by reading his profile! Sad though, that he probably doesn't know any better.

So apparently the fashion trend is to wear a snap-back hat sized to sit like a bottle cap on top of your head? Perhaps I'm just getting old and just don't understand these youngsters anymore!

DID YOU REALLY POST THAT ON YOUR PROFILE!?

Keep It Classy While I Slut-It-Up for You!

Headline: Keep it classy follow me on ig!

About Me:

Just ask. Follow me on IG [REMOVED]

PLEASE DO NOT just write HEY or WHAT'S UP! That's really boring you will get ignored.

DID YOU REALLY POST THAT ON YOUR PROFILE!?

Blogger Commentary:

This is another perfect example of a girl sending completely conflicting messages. She wants you to "keep it classy" yet she sluts it up quite nicely. Perhaps if she WAS a classy girl, she would have actually worn clothes!

Additionally, with the blatant lack of information about her in her "About Me" sections, the only thing to talk about really are her physical assets.

Daniel J Muhlestein

Take The Money And Run! FAST!!!

DID YOU REALLY POST THAT ON YOUR PROFILE!?

Education: High School

Profession: Work

About Me:

If you want to get to know me more hit me up

Blogger Commentary:

This guy is just begging to get taken! I'm quite certain that there are a few folks with just as cool nick names who would love to talk to this guy- to name a few: DEA, IRS, DHS, INS....among others.

Surely his High school guidance counselor must have informed him of IRS Form 8300: Report of Cash Payments over $10,000 Received in a Trade or Business.

As far as his "profession" is concerned "work" is also a street industry term for performing illicit tasks.

Before you date this fine young man, ladies, you may want to do a background check on him to ensure that you aren't caught in a dragnet with this guy for his felonious activities.

I would highly encourage you to use a fake name and location, and then take as many of those Benjamin's home with you as possible!!

This Is Me Showing My Best Side!

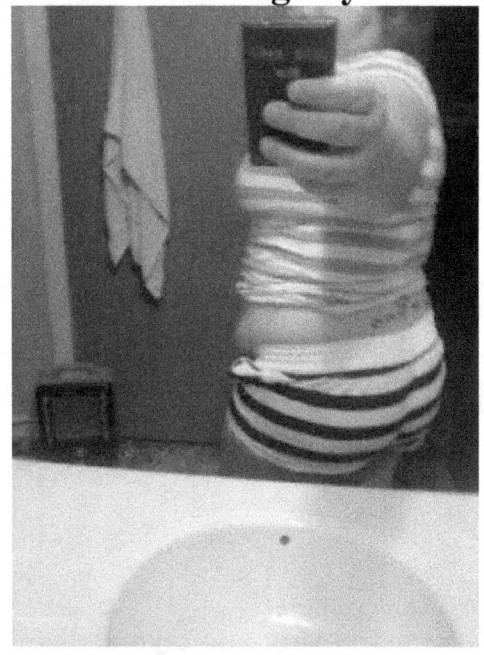

DID YOU REALLY POST THAT ON YOUR PROFILE!?

About Me:

1. i love to take care of my childed that my hobbies.

2.my golds r to find some one that i can be wifffor a long time.

3.i love to take care of kids an one day i would love to open up a nursy.

4. i love all kinds of music but my best one is rap.

First Date:

for my first date i love to eat and take walks in the park and would love to get to know that special person who ever yhu r

Blogger Commentary:

Seriously, if this is the first impression this girl wants to show a potential man, holy crap! The guy must have his "bar of standards" set to about ground level. Girl can't dress, can't write, and I'm sure the list doesn't end there! She is skilled at makin' babies at a barely legal age though! Well I suppose her dream of opening up a NURSERY may come true what with her baby makin' skills and all! And she can get it all funded by the government! - and by that I mean welfare checks!

She may want to look for a man whose first name may be Cleatus!

DID YOU REALLY POST THAT ON YOUR PROFILE!?

Not a Racist- Just Be Pink!

Headline: **Likes to be rhode hard and put up wet**

Interests:

Tats
Firm a$$s
Piercings
Breast
About Me:
Fun loving and looking for fun with wild women ... Color
is not a problem blk or white it's all pink in the middle

Blogger Commentary:

At least his dog loves him! Such a warm, welcoming look this guy has! On the positive side, at least this guy isn't a racist- his only qualification is that they be pink in the middle. I suppose that's not too much to ask these days!

Safety First! That's This Cougar's Motto- And OSHA Thanks You For That!

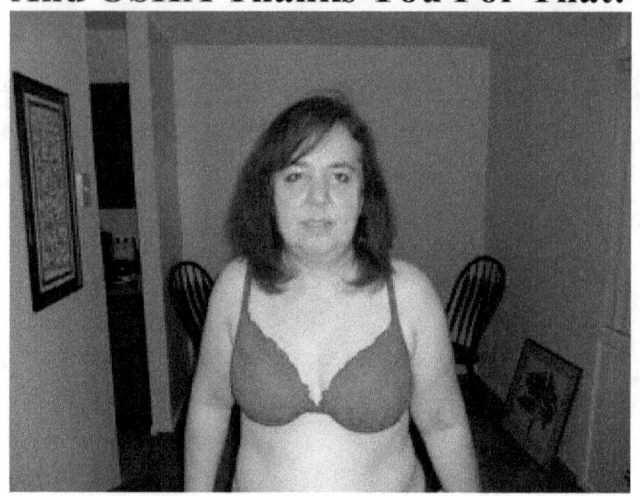

About Me:

I love to travel. Hawaii,Los Angeles and New Orleans are my favorite spots. I love the movies and go often. I love to have great conversation over coffee and love to eat out.

I am a happy positive person who loves life. Though I am not opposed to guys in their 40's I am a cougar and do prefer younger men in their 20's and 30's. Please guys, do NOT contact me if:

You don't like a girl with a big ass. I'm a sexy BBW.

You don't want to use a condom. There is too much funk out there not to be careful.

You're easily offeneded. I'm a naughty girl and love to party. If you want a good girl look under long term.

And guys if I don't get back to you right away don't think I'm ignoring you. And if you are not in [REMOVED] please don't message me unless you plan on visiting [REMOVED]. I just don't have time to chat with you unless you're local and want to hook up. I get a lot of messages and try to get back to everyone if you send me a nice message. Btw if there are any hot ladies reading this please feel free to contact me. I am curious. Also, I am just looking for fwb nsa fun. Oh, and if you're a young military guy you def have my attention. I have a thing for you military guys. m

Blogger Commentary:

Bmmpff..........Excuse me......I think I just threw up a little in my mouth! Uggggg!

In the words of Forrest Gump: That's all I have to say about that.

DID YOU REALLY POST THAT ON YOUR PROFILE!?

LOOK! Buckwheat Grew Up Into A Man-Slut!

Headline: I **am look for a big booty who love sexx**

About Me:

I Want ****n I look for friends

First Date:

Blogger Commentary:

Hey All you single ladies! It looks like Buckwheat still exists! (And from what I can tell, is in need of some MANSCAPING) He seems to have grown into quite the little slut, -but we can't really fault him for that.

DID YOU REALLY POST THAT ON YOUR PROFILE!?

She's Got Junk In The Trunk-Nothin' 'Tween The Ears!

Headline: **come and get me am weating for u boo**

About Me:

i love to go to move and to. meat new pelp in life.
am not about game.
so dont play them with me .
cuz i wont with u boo and love to meat new pelp in
[REMOVED]
or all over [REMOVED] when ever

Blogger Commentary:

I couldn't understand a damn thing this girl wrote! No matter- At least her "profile" pic looks good!

I Treat Myself like a Piece of Meat- It's probably how I'll treat You Too

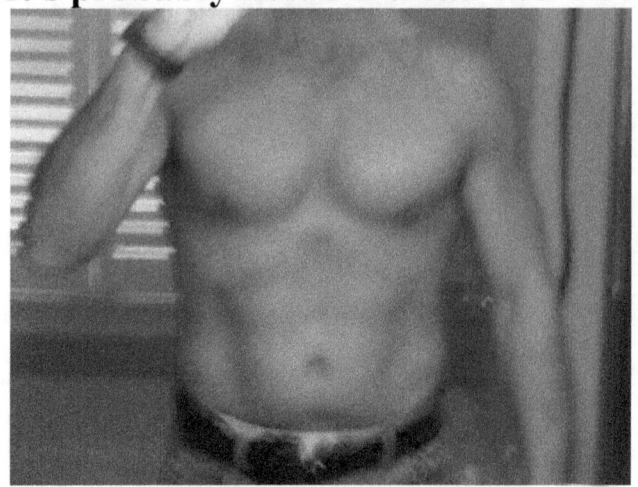

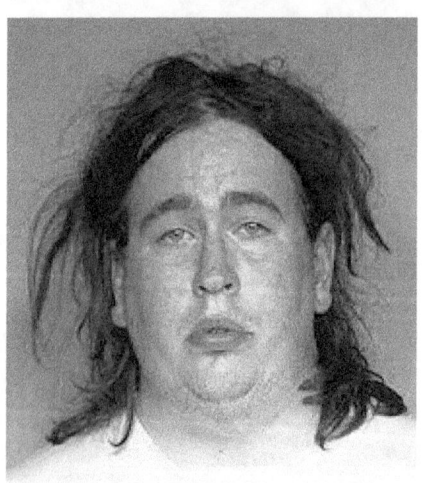

About Me:

Very Professional but also very laid back...not sweating the small stuff. Looking for an attractive woman who is sexy,confident,intelligent, self assured, strong, independent and likes to have fun...who btw is not opposed to romance and passion. Taking care of myself and staying in shape are important to me and should also be to her. I can be found at the gym 6 or 7 days a week also enjoy running 5K's. I am confident and comfortable in my own skin. Being on the beach is 1 of my favorite things. Physical attraction, chemistry and a sense of humor are a must. Love live bands and dancing so having some rhythm is helpful.

First Date:

Nothing serious maybe a drink some dancing....who knows take it from there

Blogger Commentary:

This is this guy's ONE AND ONLY photo! Just a torso-WTF? Who does this? -Oh yeah, a self-absorbed masochist.

Ladies apparently all you get in this deal is a big slab of meat. Makes you think if he treats himself like a piece of meat (as pictured here), he likely will treat you the same way. If you are cool with this, then sign yourself up!

DID YOU REALLY POST THAT ON YOUR PROFILE!?

He doesn't show his face- perhaps if his torso is his best feature, he's probably hideous! I took the creative liberty of interpreting what his face looks like (given the region of America where he lives).

P.S. He says he is a banker. Can you say MOMMY MAKEOVER!!

ENJOY!!

Daniel J Muhlestein

Uhhhhhh...Hey Beavis.......
This Chick's Coooool! ....H he he...

DID YOU REALLY POST THAT ON YOUR PROFILE!?

About Me:

I am a divorced mother of three wonderful children looking for a companion to s -pend time with and get laid. jk lol. but really... just heavy petting. I'm sick of masturbating and am seeking the real thing ;) if you can't tell, I have an excellent sense of humor. I read comic books on a daily basis LOL.

First Date

romantic walk on the beach with lots of rose pedals and maybe a candle lit dinner follwed by a board game. preferably candy land. the end.

Blogger Commentary:

I love her honesty! That's so awesome! Although I must admit that my Beavis and Butt Head alter ego kicked in there for a while and had fun with the word play in her profile!

Ya know, and if she is a comic book geek, she just may enjoy hanging out with the guy below her. (When I say "hanging out with" I mean, full financial support and housing of that guy). -Who knows it could work! I'm sure that he's pretty skilled at what she likes to do too. -Just Sayin'

I Call It MARKET RESEARCH....
You Call It Living In My Parents Basement

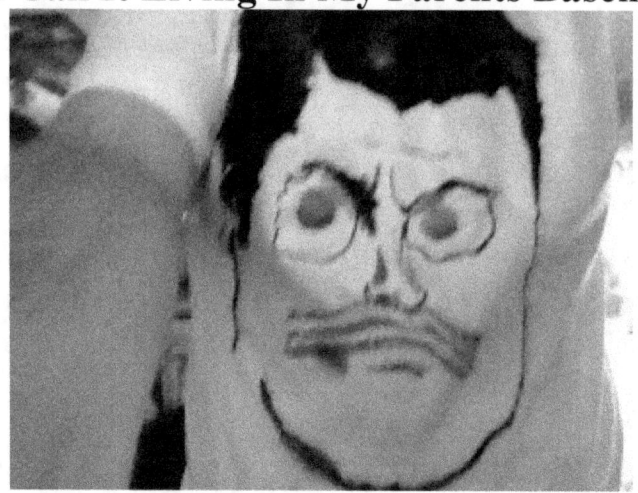

Profession: Market Research

About Me:

I work from home where I conduct market research. I'm also an avid collector and dealer of vintage video games, video tapes, records, toys and other odds and ends. I like to cook curries and stews and soups. My favorite band at the moment is Coheed & Cambria.

Blogger Commentary:

Profession: Market Research- By "market research" I mean I surf Google all day long!

DID YOU REALLY POST THAT ON YOUR PROFILE!?

About Me:

I work from home where I conduct market research. (By this he means that he lives in his parent's basement surfing Google all day long) I'm also an avid collector and dealer of vintage video games, video tapes, records, toys and other odds and ends. (By this he means that he has EVERY gaming system known to man, and enjoys playing them all day in his parent's basement.) I like to cook curries and stews and soups. My favorite band at the moment is Coheed & Cambria

Awww, It's the boy who refuses to grow up and be a real man. He still collects his toys and video games thinking that someday this eclectic collection of his will someday make him RICH! And then he will have the last laugh on the world!

He is the type of guy who is always frustrated because he is SO MISUNDERSTOOD! If people could just see the world through HIS eyes! Uhhhhh....Sorry to burst your bubble there bud, but we did see the world through your eyes, and then we stopped at the age of around 16 and a half. - which is where we finally realized no one will take us seriously by playing with our childhood toys, living in our parents basement playing video games all day and calling it market research.

You Just Got TOLD Boyz!!

About Me:

I am a transplant from up north .I am an outgoing,straight
to the point,caring and very affectionate female. I am
looking for a grown-ass MAN that is living like a man.
Someone that I can have fun with I hate "dry" uptight ppl.
I love to laugh. The sexiest thing to me is a funny man. Ii
want a sensual ,sexy man that is attentive to me and not
just assume I like what otherwomen like. Im
confused..why are some of you using the "long term"
profile to get sex? Really though sir?? Im not at all
interested in being anyone's booty call or side piece. Also
fellas if I cant physically speak to u and u.are a serial texter

DID YOU REALLY POST THAT ON YOUR PROFILE!?

ummm... figure it out that I AM NOT gonna talk to u for a week via text..control,alt delete. Why is asking for sane,normal and no behavioral health issues like pulling teeth? Some of these folk are damn crazy..smh..look fellas not tryna b funny but...if u r any of the following.....gay,bi,tri=tryin shit,married,attached,engaged,baby mamma drama,stalkers etc.. Please miss me wit alll that!

And last but not least if you dont have time,got game and other sh*t with u please dont waste my time or yours..

Update: Fellas, if one more person ask me for an ass shot ima cuss! I mean really? If the size of my ass is a determining factor or a dealbreaker I dont want to deal with u no way. What if I was the type to ask for a pic of your "piece" and it wasnt what im used to..should that b a dealbreaker sir? Hmm? I hear crickets..and dammit! Ppl weed ,dippers,pcp,reefer,loud,pacqiou,purp,haze,boat whatever ur drug of choice is called in ur neck of the damn woods PSA: ITS A DRUG! CHECK YES U DO DRUGS ! IF I MEET ONE MORE DAMN POTHEAD /DIPPERHEAD SMH..

Now I kinda see why some of u are single..focused on the wrong stuff to base a relationship on.

And some of yall..smfh..stop acting like u are hard up for sex we all know u can get sex when u cant get a sandwich..if u cant then idk what to tell u..its not the end of the world I see alot of u want respectful women..well how respectful is that to spread eagle on the first date? Make up your mind half the time I dont even think some of yall know what yall want because some of the messages ive been getting .....*blankstare* im just gon say "oh you TRIED IT! and with that being said if you cant send a respectful message sit down and have a few seats until you realize how to address a lady,please & thank you

Blogger Commentary:

I'm adding this profile because I really love it! Yes the grammar is horrendous, but I was actually laughing out loud while reading this! Any guy who reads this profile

JUST GOT TOLD! I can only imagine the dating horror stories this woman has gone through! I mean, I have heard some doosies, but I have a feeling this woman could shock me to a whole new level with her dating stories!

Love this woman!!

DID YOU REALLY POST THAT ON YOUR PROFILE!?

Objects In The Rear View Mirror May Seem Closer Than They Appear.....STALKER!!!

Blogger Commentary:

This is the best profile photo this guy could come up with? Perhaps if he looks best in his rear view mirror, maybe you should leave him in YOUR rear view mirror! What the hell are people thinking anymore?

I Wasn't Born This Way......

About Me:

I'm a different person....Firstly, I'm a pre-op transexual, not a born female. I am an entertainer as well. I live here in [REMOVED], and been hurt a number of times, but that hurt has turned me into the beautiful person I am today! Do not waste time because life is too short.... You should message me if you are interested, and let's see where it goes.... I am looking for a relationship but its doesn't have to be the topic of conversation.

DID YOU REALLY POST THAT ON YOUR PROFILE!?

First Date:

I just wanna be able to be me..... If he's down ,and can accept that, then we're in business!

Blogger Commentary:

I think I just found a date for the guy below this girl! I think they would be great together :)

Says: "I'm a different person...." YOU CAN SAY THAT AGAIN!!

"I'm an entertainer" - I'm sure this one is HIGHLY entertaining to be around!!

Good luck to whoever dates this one!!

50 Shades of Grey?
(He Would Like To Think So)
WARNING! EXPLICIT CONTENT!!

Headline: **rub my lips on it kiss both thighs**

About Me:

what i said and do on my page is me and how i feel if i speak or say something to u dont mean i want you am going to say do what i feel on my page u dont like kick a wheel am doing me i like to have fun express my self

First Date:

Cradled between your tender thighs
I lift you to my mouth.
The abundance of your wetness greets me
and my mouth overflows with your warm essence.
Your sweet taste is on my tongue
and your fragrance delights my senses.
No gentle lick this visit.
No bashful cautious approach
For I wish to consume you.

DID YOU REALLY POST THAT ON YOUR PROFILE!?

Push against my hungry mouth
As the tip of my tongue slides up the slippery furrow
that welcomes me between rows of delicate pink petals.
Thrust against my generous tongue.

Show me the power of your desire
for my oral caress.
My exploring tongue lifts the hood
and finds your smooth firm pearl.
You squeal in that unique way,
signaling that I have found your special spot.
I harden in response.

My jaws protests what my open mouth provides
but I am unrelenting in my gift,
intent only on your fulfillment.
I feel your body tense,
and you are quiet now...
Concentrating... bearing down.
Soon now my love,
ecstasy approaches.

You push hard and fast against my tongue,
shameless in using me
and I so willingly comply
until you cry out...
and in your satisfaction,
I will find mine,
But mine will be the greater.

Blogger Commentary:

This guy I believe fancies himself as a "Christian Grey" from the "mommy porn" series: 50 Shades of Grey.

He apparently has nothing else to offer you other than quotes from an adult novel he picked up somewhere, and his wannabe LL Cool J lip lick.

WHAT AN IDIOT!! lol.

DID YOU REALLY POST THAT ON YOUR PROFILE!?

Unhappily Married-
Seeking Friends with Benefits

Stats:

Marital Status: Married

About Me:

I am fun loving, confident, sexy and I have a heart larger than life. I am brutally honest, so if you do not like that, move on. I am in a marriage that I am not happy with, just because I'm here does not mean I'm a slut or a whore, I just need that void in my life filled. Looking for one person to be my FWB.

First Date:

Somewhere public with no expectations for anything more than good conversation and go from there.

Blogger Commentary:

OK fellas' check your moral compass at the door to wrap your mind around this one! She's looking for FWB (Friends With Benefits).

With an unhappy wife usually comes an unhappy husband, you might want to watch your back on this one too.

4 Rednecks and a 4-Wheeler....
What Every Girl Has Always Dreamed Of!

Stats:

Drinks more than 3 times a week.

About Me:

Hello!!! I am 25 years old like to go out and party with all my friends. I am into outdoors activities bonfires, fourwheelers, off roading, and hunting I'm a bit of a country boy. Recently bought a house that I share with my big American bulldog diesel. I find this site to be a little creepy and funny. Well i guess if ya want to know anything else hit me up. I think its just easier for the girl to start the convo since im sure all the ladies get a sh*t ton of perverted messages from some weirdos.

First Date:

Depends on the girl and the time of the year. With some nice weather I would like to go out and do something fun!

Blogger Commentary:

Which one of the 4 rednecks on this 4-wheeler is this profile referring to? Perhaps this is one of those "I drink more than 3 times a week" photo-ops! This could be a preview of what your first date may be like. -You, 3 of his redneck buddies, and an abused 4-wheeler!!

DID YOU REALLY POST THAT ON YOUR PROFILE!?

Gentlemen Only-
Even If I Wear the Uniform of a Slut

Profession: Tease

About Me:

looking for someone to have fun with nothing serious I enjoy my job hiking shopping and relaxing with a glass of wine by a pool .. can you be a gentleman?

Blogger Commentary:

So she's asking for her guy to be a "gentleman" when she's wearing the uniform of a slut. -Kind of a conflict of interest wouldn't you think? As you can see in this photo she is accentuating her finest assets.

Her profession is listed as "Tease," again, here we go with the conflict of interest if she is seeking to be treated like she is requesting.

Perhaps before beginning this date, you may want to have her sign a liability waiver, to ensure everyone is legally covered from any misinterpretations of the messages she is sending.

DID YOU REALLY POST THAT ON YOUR PROFILE!?

Look Everyone, Eor Is a Real Person!!

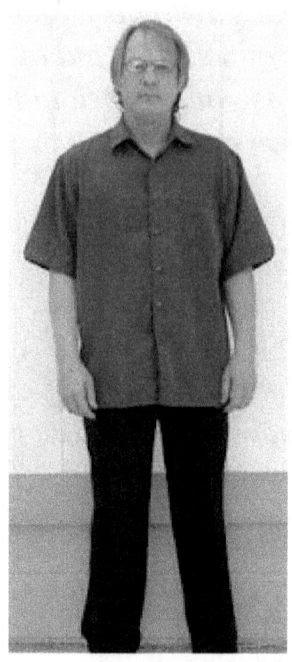

I am a kind, caring person. I am not the most motivated person anymore, but I try. I like music. I play the guitar, but am quite rusty at it. I used to sing too, but my voice has deteriorated for some unknown reason.

Blogger Commentary:

Look ladies, it's the live version of Eor the donkey! And this guy kinda looks like the embodiment of Eor too!

The Next Beyoncé You Are NOT!

Stats:

Perfers not to say if she drinks or not

Profession: RN

Headline: ***~Time: live it, Date: fuk it~*•**

About Me:

I guess some men dont know wen dey got sumthin good...I am very loyal and trust worthy. I like to draw, play video games, kickn it. my goals r to graduate n get my degree n

RN n to go back to skoo fo anesthesiologist n i wnt to own a business later in life.i am very determined.i am nice, sweet, loving,cn b cold hearted, complicated sumtimes. i love to read n i like all music except fo certain stuff. i like all cultures n i love to learn about different cultures as well even der language. i am black, italian,indian, etc.

Blogger Commentary:

From my experiences in writing this blog, it has been a recurring pattern that any woman in the nursing profession seems to be straight out of the "hood," and all wanna-be-gangsta! Maybe I should never go to a hospital EVER if this trend seems to continue.

Note to future employers: This is a prime example of why you would want to check a job candidates social media pages prior to hiring them. - Very scary.....

Uhhhhhhhhhh..........?????????? What?

Stats: 60 yrs. old.

Headline: **Liberal Progressive Free Thinker seeking**

About Me:

The headline explains a lot. It's not something easy to find with all the conservative-inspired fear and hysteria that's out there. So if you're a fan of Glen or Rush, move on, please. If you're more concerned with money than people, well, keep looking. If you think corporations are people — hey, show me their birth certificates, why don't you. Oh, and I want ALL my personal relationships to be with a person, here, and now.

I like having a full life. However, this fullness includes time spent with someone who is both endearing and companionable. I've met some very nice people over time. But so far the connection I'm looking for hasn't materialized. The efforts have been honest but have yielded no fruit. It's all about the connection, for me. I also believe that it's not something easily revealed quickly. The true nature of a relationship is brewed over time. The quality of a relationship is revealed over time. It's much like stock simmering on the stove — the longer it simmers the more its essence is released. Unfortunately, perhaps for me, so many people want to move quickly. I've found that path just doesn't work for me. I want to spend time getting to know someone, one step at a time. While I haven't connected with the love I'd follow to the ends of the earth (wait, did I say that out loud?) I have found some good friends.

As I tell everyone "I live alone." (It's a standard gag.) My only child is living in [REMOVED] after graduating college. She's taking some time off before going off to grad school. My little house in this quiet neighborhood is rather empty. My time is filled with taking care of all the gardens and the house itself. I bought the place because it needed little work compared to the old house in Uptown. However, I didn't factor in the time required to tend the 11 gardens.

DID YOU REALLY POST THAT ON YOUR PROFILE!?

Sometimes I think a 55 gallon drum of Treflan would be just about right.

I've always got some project going on. I'm not terribly good at sitting still. I tend to do things, make things, learn things instead. I don't care for television. I've spent more than 30 years in the media of one form or another and personally I'd much rather read or do something else instead of sitting in front of the tube. Of course that doesn't dismiss the collection of movies downstairs--that's another case altogether.

I'm originally from [REMOVED]. I've been here for many years now, having come out here for college; then leaving and returning several times. At one point I spent about a year living in France. The rest of my family is still on the [REMOVED].

I like to cook when I have someone to cook for. Yes, I can actually do more than push buttons on a microwave. I seek intelligent conversation, and believe in reason and thoughtfulness. I can be exacting but I am fiercely loyal and supportive. I take my work seriously but don't take myself very seriously at all. I'm interested in being with someone kind and compassionate and genuine--someone soft, and gentle and understanding who prefers to be a partner in all things. Life hasn't always been easy, but I see no point in making it any harder than need be.

I'm proudly liberal. I care about people, their (our) well being. I have little patience with prying self important busy bodies who concern themselves with only money.

Music? I actually don't listen to music all that much. I listen to a tremendous number of audiobooks. At that some time I have an oddly eclectic collection of music I've picked up from around to world. It ranges from Western European classical to drum sets from Africa, pop tunes from Spain, Italian opera, singer/songwriter pieces from all over, folk music from the 60s, well, lots from the 60s (and no, I don't remember all of the 60s), and more traditional music from the Andes to Ireland and the island to the east of it.

So that's probably enough for now. More comes with conversation. I'm a rather retiring type, so it takes a bit to get out of my shell. But once I do you'd never know that I was ever shy in the first place.

Oh yeah, among other things, I spend some time on boats.

First Date:

I actually enjoy going out to eat. It gives us a chance to sit and relax, have a little something to eat and get to know each other a little. I enjoy good food and small quiet restaurants. I even enjoy cooking, but only if there's someone else to cook for.

DID YOU REALLY POST THAT ON YOUR PROFILE!?

Blogger Commentary:

Zzzzzzzzzzzzzzzzzzzzzzzzzzzzzzzzzzzzzz............Oh, OK. You're done reading his manifesto. Whew! This guy is a whole different brand of freaky weird! Holy crap!

Good luck with this guy ladies!!

Sharing Is Caring...Right?

Stats: Married.

About Me:

Happily married in an open marriage. Looking for new friends and people to hang out with. Looking for new experiences.

Blogger Commentary:

Uhhhhh......She should totally contact the devil in the post below her! -Just sayin'......

Forget 50 Shades Of Grey...More Like 50 Reasons To Run Away!!

Are you interested in hanging out, playing pool, having fun, NSA sex, swingers' clubs, swingers' vacations, etc?

How about jumping out of planes, getting in the car and heading to parts unknown on a whim, scuba diving? What

DID YOU REALLY POST THAT ON YOUR PROFILE!?

about engaging in various forms of fornication & copulation while doing them?

If you're not scared, and can really be a NSA or FWB, let's do it!!!

Blogger Commentary:

Uhhhhhh......This guy looks like the devil! Is this his "trust me, I'm safe" look? I have no problem with people who want to live the swinger lifestyle- It's their own business among consenting adults. This guy DOES NOT put the "Grrrrrrrrrr" in SWINGER. (That's Austin Power's job). This guy puts the "911.... I'm about to be assaulted and raped!" in swinger.

Even Flavor Flav Is Wondering W.T.F. !?

Headline: **BADD B*TCH!**

Stats: Drinks more than 3 times a week.

Profession: Customer service representative

DID YOU REALLY POST THAT ON YOUR PROFILE!?

About Me:

I love to chill wit my daughta, my goal is to open my own hair salon.. Ima down ass females, if you keep it G wit me, ill keep it G witchu.. I like rap, hip hop, r&b, slow jams.. I love basketball & football.. 76ers & da Eagles..

First Date:

Our first date we could go to eat then to the movies then back to my krib & sip on a lil sumthin

Blogger Commentary:

I think this girl was probably rejected to be on the reality show "Flavor of Love" with Flavor Flav (pictured above). I think they would make a cute couple though.

So This Is How Successful Dream Chasin' N****s Pose?

Headline: **Just a hood Nigga Chasing his dreams....**

Stats: Smokes occasionally, Does drugs socially,

Profession: Football

DID YOU REALLY POST THAT ON YOUR PROFILE!?

About Me:

I'm a sinner who probably going to sin again loud forgive me for things I don't understand. Sometimes I got be alone **** don't kill my Vibe. [REMOVED] NFL follow the journey

First Date:

Just have to wait and find out

Blogger Commentary:

I think we gotta get this guy hooked up with Tony Robbins or somethin' He's OBVIOUSLY a professional football player- because that's what he put for his profession. It appears he has the party life of a football star nailed, just not the skill part that got the football star to where they are.

He has the dream, but it seems hasn't done anything to actually realize it. He smokes a lot of weed (I'm assuming) but keeps saying. I'll work out on the field tomorrow.

I kinda feel bad for this kid. Maybe he just needs an intervention instead of an interception!

Goldilocks Has Turrets!

Blogger Commentary:

What The Hell?? What was this woman thinking posting this pic on her profile? Are "crazy eyes" the new vogue fashion where she's from? To be fair, she may have had one of her fake eye lashes fall into her eye causing extreme irritation just as the photo snapped. -It could happen. Perhaps she just has an extreme case of Turrets Syndrome- in which case, we shouldn't make fun. (I apologize)

You Too Can Be A White Dot In His Next Profile Pic!

Blogger Commentary:

This guy screams CLASS! Most of his profile photos had women's faces with white dots over them. It's as though he has no friends to take an actual photo of just himself, and he isn't able to operate the camera to take a cheesy bathroom mirror shot or something?

Ladies, if you're looking for the "white dot" treatment, this is your guy!

Stepford Wife Turned Alcoholic

Blogger Commentary:

This woman should have maybe thought twice about posting this "wine tasting" photo on her dating profile! It makes her appear somewhat like a "stay-at-home-lush." She also has kind of the " XANAX'ed-out" peaceful look on her face. But perhaps it's the 10 glasses of wine she's about to slam!

DID YOU REALLY POST THAT ON YOUR PROFILE!?

I'll take you Home in My Tractor!

Stats:

Smokes often

Drinks more than 3 times a week

Likes Fishing, Video Games, Movies

About Me:

I work full time. I've got a great job, my own truck and place. I work drink and play video games, and that's how I spend my time. I'm looking for new things to do. I enjoy fishing in the summer, bowling with friends playing pool and just having a good time.

Blogger Commentary:

Ladies here we have the Ubiquitous "guy posing with a fish" profile photo! You have got to love the little extra splash of class he adds with the cigarette dangling from his mouth!

I'm not sure if men come more "basic" than this guy, based on his profile and his likes. If you want to explore your true inner redneck, this guy may just be for you!

I Got Gangsta' Bedside Skills- Cuz Ima CNA

Profession: CNA,CNA,CNA FOR THOSE WHO DNT FOLLOW CNA!!!

Education: Graduate degree

About Me: Im not the average pls trust tht... Dnt play ya self anyway im very smart and so is my mouth i hate bullsh*t i ddnt play games as a child i was a Doll kinda girl so i refuse to play em in my adult life im looking for a grown ass man! In every sense of the word not a "Date" i want that if i can't sleep he knws wat to say to help me relax kinda of man for the pervs (NOT PHONE SEX) eww i wna grow to want him cause i have no choice he makes me feel that good about me kinda man i'm a CNA i have one child i gave birth to. i have TWO BOYS I ADOPTED no i dont club nope dont smoke weed i drink maybe twice a month i eat lobster 3x a week THERE!!!!! Dnt ask me much more oh... And pls just cause u msg me dnt mean i wna tlk to

Blogger Commentary:

Graduate degree huh? I'm assuming from "McUniversity" based on her amazing grammar skills. Works in the nursing field? Like so many other "nurses" on this blog, please steer clear from anywhere they work!

N***a PLEASE.........Don't Ask Me Out!

Stats: Occasional smoker with average body type
Education: Some university
Profession: SportinG Goods * Money***
About Me:
1st ima start by saying i aint on this sh*t24/7, Niggas be on
here cuz they thirsty and i aint with that. 2nd i aint gunna
put my whole info up bcuz niggas on here are just noisy,
and tryna stalk ppl.
2nd. Ima cool ,sweetheart,loyal ass nigga , cant tell that i
am?? hmu then. See whats behind my my life not just by
lookiing at how niggas look in pictures dont waste yur
time trust me. If theres real females out there , not phony
ass chicks whos gunna just talk to. Mad niggas lmao bcuz
ikno alot of chicks who i had a conversation with and not

just with me, even with my niggas on here to and be tryna play both sides, nha i aint with that. Iknow a fake when i see on. But like i said msg. Me to know about me cuz i aint gunna put it up!!

8 figure deal figure

NO FAKES, hmu ON [REMOVED]!

Im that Loyal Nigga!

[REMOVED]

If yu real my Fb- [REMOVED] So Appalled

IG- Show [REMOVED] thot

Blogger Commentary:

Occasional smoker= likes the 420, the Kush, Maui Wowi, Pineapple Express.

His profession? Probably sales associate at Foot Locker-MAYBE!

Says he has some university. Where the hell are these people going to college that teaches them to write this way? (This is a repeating theme on this blog)

His pervasive use of the "N" word. WTF man? If I, as a white guy, can't "acceptably" use that word, then you shouldn't either. Have some respect for your race! I believe these are also the same people who are always pulling the "race card" when things don't go their way. Well no shit man! Perhaps it's because you are a fucking idiot! -And apparently proud of it, and expect the world to embrace your ignorance. NO THANKS! (Anyway, I digress)

DID YOU REALLY POST THAT ON YOUR PROFILE!?

This one seems a bit accustomed to the "face forward, then side profile" photos made popular in detention centers.

Ok ladies, you probably want to do a background check on this guy first- If you get stopped by police and he has outstanding warrants (something tells me he may have them), It could ruin a fabulous first date with this guy.

Two Heads Are Better Than One?

About Me/Us:
Hello hello there, our names are [REMOVED] and [REMOVED] We are best friends! And we love each other so much and know we want each other in our lives but we still need that "male anatomy part" ;) so basically we are trying to see if any of you men would be interested

in having a relationship with two girls :) we know this all sounds crazy, but hey anything is possible these days, just message us and we'll see what happens :)

Blogger Commentary:
Oh MY! Just when I thought I saw it all!
Synonyms for what you get here:
BOGO (Buy One, Get One)
A Two-Fer (2 for one)
A 2-4-1
Two Heads Are Better Than One
The More The Merrierer
Double Down
Double Coupon Days
Sandwiched
Scissors lock
-Your fantasy fulfilled!

Morning Wood and Overly Confident

About Me:
look if you aren't what you say you are then don't bother me I wiil see through it quickly. if your pics are taken wile you were in high school and you no longer loo like that example (like if you done had kids and blew up 50 lbs or have stretch marks that you could have avoided by simply getting off your fat lazy ass and getting some good lotion . that sh*tmakes me want to throw up . I don't like being shallow or mean but I've met some real pretty girls that were either , liars , stripers , flat out psychotic still have not met any one that is mature and successful enough to be around me with out being to jealous or insecure to get any more of my extrs time , I just moved up to [] on the 1st of November 2012 , I really enjoy physical exercise ,

mma, boxing , eating any thing I can get my hand on . and wile we are on the subject of eating wink wink , eating at the Y is something I enjoy on a more personal note. a hole lot it really turns me on but you have to be very attractive and must take good care of yourself physically and medically must stay very clean another words .and if you are a stripper that is not a deal breaker , just cant be a ragging slut , and damn sure don't try to lie to me about being a stripper I will see right thru it as I have several time over the at least 12 years on the road / you all have the same issue mentally , and have at least 85 % of the same personality trait s but hey feel free to try to prove me wrong. I must warn you I can be very addicting physically and will have you wondering how I do that . oh yaw I've seen some of the douche bags that are suppose to be my competition im as real as it gets . no games no gimmicks I m the one in the pics , I don't drink often because of the fact that it is terrible for both mind body and soul . a women that is close to god is a very large plus , so im threw being a ***hole so if you like what you see and hear then lets grab some good food may ab beer or two . and go from their , I also like to snow board so that would be cool to . and if you don't want to meet up after a few phone conversations for stupid reasons I will block your number , and you profile I have face book under [REMOVED] if you want to authenticate that I am real that is cool just click on friends lol , most of all don't waste my time , other than that ,GO FISHIN HAHA ;]

DID YOU REALLY POST THAT ON YOUR PROFILE!?

Blogger Commentary:

Wow this guy is something else! Did he just say: "eating at the Y is something I enjoy" for the uninitiated out there, that's a term used for the act of cunnilingus (I'll not explain further).

This guy makes himself out to be God's gift to women. -I think it may be the 'roids talken' there buddy. Judging by the way he writes (if you want to call it writing), He is a complete idiot, and is placing all his bets that his chiseled look will get him by. - Apparently he has lots of experiences with strippers since he purports to know the inner-workings of the stripper's mind. Perhaps strippers are who he needs to stick with; they seem to be on the same level mentally, as well as in the vanity DPT.

An Obvious Graduate Of
"How to Win Friends and Influence People"

Headline: ***Idgaf bout your opinion I pose 4 da camera ;).**

About Me:

FIRST OFF : THIS FOR U DUMB DUDES WHO R
SADDEN CAUSE I DON'T WANNA **** BUDDY LOL
I DON'T CARE BOUT UR OUTLOOK ON MY DRESS
IN MY PHOTOS, I DON'T STEP OUT ON THE
STREETS LIKE THAT I ONLY POSE FOR THE
CAMERA !!IT'S FRIGGIN SNOWING OUTSIDE I
WALK RIUND THE HOUSE N SHORTS NOT
OUTSIDE !!! DUMB ASS'S I SWEAR ... LOL

DID YOU REALLY POST THAT ON YOUR PROFILE!?

I DONT WANT ANY OF YALLS****! & If you come at me saying you wanna do this & that too me you will be IGNORED !
SECOND: I'm not looking for a **** buddy, I want to fellowship wit someone who's on my level .
THIRD:.If yous a broke dude & can't spend them dollars then kick rocks cause I'm high maintenance & deserves nothing bt the best...
Nickname [REMOVED] , I love pit bulls I'm twenty years old so I do occasionally like to go to the club & dance .
I listen gospel , hip hop & r&b soul music . I listen to some alternative music depending on the artists. Graduated from highsxhool in 2010 . I like to go to the movies hang out. & adore shopping .... I do like to smoke kush from time to time wt my ladies ... My career path is in the nursing field .Im looking for someone who wants ah serious relationship eventually . If your not about that life don't waste ur time cause I don't want YOUR****!
First Date:
Someone I can take n public to dinner & a movie .

Blogger Commentary:

This girl is one hot mess! She goes from shouting in all caps, to her wanna-be gangsta' speak. Her career path is in the nursing field? I need to get the name of whatever hospital or clinic she is working at - SO THAT I CAN AVOID IT AT ALL COSTS! The medical industry shouldn't trust her with a bottle of aspirin, let alone someone's life!

She state's that she's a high maintenance girl; hold on to your wallets boys, this one's expensive! She admits that she likes to smoke Kush (weed). Last I checked her state still considers such a thing illegal, and I seriously doubt she has a glaucoma condition with a medical marijuana card.

Gangsta' Smoove Talkin'.......

Profession: Whatever it takes to maintain
About Me:
Wuz up..I really don't like these things I feel they take away from the convo..but whatever you know message me
First Date:
I'd rather not dwell on the past

DID YOU REALLY POST THAT ON YOUR PROFILE!?

Blogger Commentary:

Let's start with his "profession" - "Whatever it takes to maintain." So ladies, what does this tell us? He's a Pimp? A dealer? Perhaps a sex worker himself? Nonetheless, it's likely Ill-gotten-gains.

This poor young man also seems to have very poor reading comprehension. He was thinking that when asked about "First Date" he thought they were asking about HIS first date. -Which apparently didn't go well according to his answer.
Good luck ladies! -Wait, this one probably doesn't date "ladies." Bring on the BITCHES AN DA HOES!

Dude Looks Like A Lady!

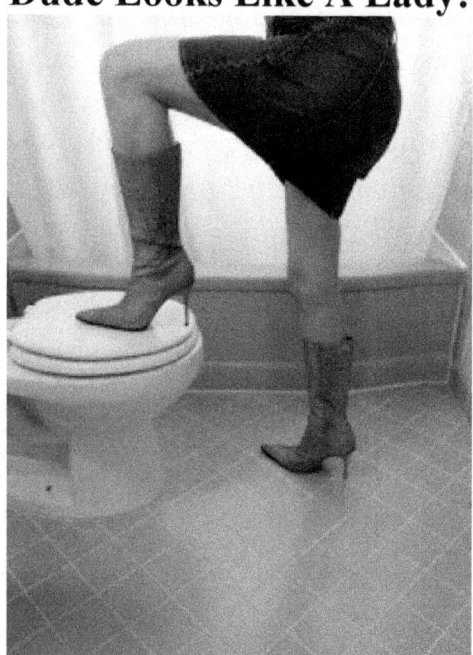

Blogger Commentary:

Ok, So I did a small experiment with my "female" profile that I use to check out the D-Bag men that I add on this blog. I happen to sell women's clothing and shoes on eBay, so I had some product lying around. I keep getting requests for my photo on my female profile. So a friend of mine and I suited me up in a skirt and some boots, I posed, and she snapped the photo. I posted it to my profile, and IMEDIATELY my In Box was blowing up! I posted below the responses I got within having the photo up for just 20 minutes!

Can I say that men have just proven that they really are douche bags! I being a guy myself (posing with some

DID YOU REALLY POST THAT ON YOUR PROFILE!?

mighty fine legs in this pic) am quite disgusted with the men on these sites! On my legitimate dating profile, I would never have said such things to women. I must say that there was only one sincere man who posted on this particular experiment- I didn't post his comment, since we're not mocking decent guys.

Hello, 35/m here in [REMOVED] Just move from Phoenix to be a partner in a small business. I am 6'1, dark hair, blue eyes, bearded and tattooed. I love women your age, I have since I was very young when I was trained by an older woman and a woman your age. I am looking for a open minded sexual woman. A woman who would love to be spoiled with whatever she would like. I would love to chat. I have a pic I can email if you are interested.
So I've been reading and rereading your profile trying to come up with something witty or funny to say to you but I have to admit I'm speechless. I decided to make it simple - you are a very beautiful woman and from what I can read I would enjoy getting to know you.

Well my name is [REMOVED] think you have a sexy pair legs sorry that I'm not LDS. I do drink so we probably wouldn't get along

I love your legs too;) GRRReat!

Wow sweet boots
Awesome legs!

You do have amazing legs I must say that.. Your profile matches those legs....

Howdy legs

I would like to be at your feet to look up those legs, wow they are really nice!!!

Love the pic. Great idea.

love your legs too! wowza!

me too lol.. *(The caption under the photo is "I Love My Legs" two hours later he posts:)* sorry that was lame

Very nice legs actually..:)

Wow!!!!! I love your legs too!!!!!

Please have more pictures! Lol

You sound yummyyy

I Love your legs too

u need to change ur pic no one can c your face.

DID YOU REALLY POST THAT ON YOUR PROFILE!?

I must say, those are pretty spectacular legs:-) the boots are awesome too!

you have a very nice toilet   so do you have a face to go with those legs

Nice bunz =)

Hello

Well hello how are U doing ? I'm [REMOVED] a great guy here looking for a great women to get to know. So if U would like to get to know a great guy ? Message me back. Hope to hear from U..

Nice legs...

Nice legs. How are you this morning

Nice legs ;)

...Lookin' To Tap Dat....

About Me:

I'm good with my hands & gentle with hearts. =-) Kid-tested & single-mom approved... In fact, I'm magnetic to cats,dogs,kids, & neighborhood-experts (especially when I'm changing my oil or merely washing the windows, or open the hood to add... fluids... In public, I'm a quiet, shy observer; but with friends I have a dry, dead-on sense of humor.. I'm cautious & careful in everything I do, but I'm also told that I'm a tender & attentive lover, making the moments last, hoping to make the most of the many moments ;-P I enjoy a simple life; to watch TV/snack in bed, fly my radio-controlled airplane, or get close to nature, (without roughing it)... ;-P I can cook a little, & I don't mind helping with the dishes, etc. NO Sports, NO hunting & NO Horror flicks!!

DID YOU REALLY POST THAT ON YOUR PROFILE!?

Blogger Commentary:

No sports, No hunting, No horror flicks? Well that eliminates pretty much anyone who likes to have sex while watching slasher flicks! Damn and I think there is someone on this blog who is into that!

The "kid-tested & single mom approved" line screams of CREEPER!

...."I'm also told that I'm a tender & attentive lover, making the moments last"....I'm not sure if this guy has many "moments" left on this earth. He may want to consult with his doctor to see if he is well enough for sexual activity- then just stick to "quickies." -Why risk it with the savoring of those long lasting moments?
He also forgot to mention AARP approved!

This Is How We Say Hello in Bitch-Topia

About Me:
My name is [REMOVED]
I enjoy reading shitty novels
and riding my bike.
I like to drink wine and get rowdy with my friends.
To me, the most attractive quality is kindness.
I'm looking for new people and new experiences.
Also, I love all things green (:
** Its annoying that I even have to say this but if all you
have up say to me is " Hey baby / Hey sexy/ sup." it's safe
to say I won't reply. Also, if you feel the need to ask me if
I'm "dtf," don't. The answer is no.**
First Date:
No Pressure (:

DID YOU REALLY POST THAT ON YOUR PROFILE!?

Blogger Commentary:

You gotta love the "One Finger and A Fist" salute she is flashing in the mirror! -Just wants to make you take her home to momma!

What You See Is What You Get -Seriously, THAT'S IT. Nothing More.

Stats:
Occasional smoker with athletic body type
Isn't seeking a relationship or any kind of commitment
Intrests:
Snowboarding, Hunting, Gym, Working on my truck

About Me:
hi, my names [REMOVED] im 24 and in decent shape. i like going snowboarding, working on my truck and going out hunting. not much else really to say im pretty simple.
First Date:
[BLANK]

Blogger Commentary:

Ahhhh...what to say about this piece of work....It seems the deepest thing about this guy may be his muscle tone. I'm quite sure that his beer sitting in front of him may have more flavor than him.

So ladies, suit yourself up for a fabulous night of talking about rock-hard abs, the complex tastes of diet beer, about the size of his engine block, the shredding runs he had on his snowboard, the biggest moose he had EVER seen, and damnit, I woulda' bagged it if only it was moose hunting season! Oh yeah, and an endless stream of tasteless military humor.

All I See Are Twin Peaks....

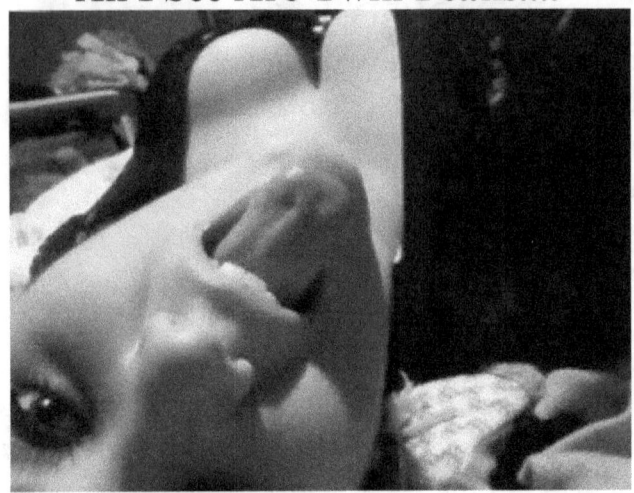

Screen Name: **[REMOVED]**
Profession: **Barbie Doll**
About Me:
What what. what. what....What what. what. what.
Hii :) my name is [REMOVED] im just on here to meet
cool people like myself and BS. ima pretty busy girl and
dont get on here much but dont be afraid to message me
anytime and ill get back to ya as soon as i can. :) later
gator.
First Date:
Well nothin' ha. but im good a beerpong if ya need a
partner :).

Blogger Commentary:

*This particular post is slightly different than my typical
post in that this one has its own brand of "WTF?" She*

certainly loves to accentuate her positive features- and for that, we thank you!

She says that she is a pretty busy girl; I have a strange feeling that she spends a lot of time just lying around on her back with her heels kicked to the ceiling. When she's not busy on her back, she's up for a killer game of beer-pong! –A sporty woman, we like those too!

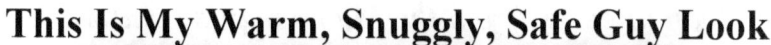

This Is My Warm, Snuggly, Safe Guy Look

Headline: **lookin for a nice woman that don't care**
Stats:
30 yrs old, drinks at least 3 times a week, longest relationship was less than a year long, works as sales associate at a discount store.
About Me:
hows it going you can call me [REMOVED].not much to tell bout me i'm turning a new leaf on life.but feel free to

DID YOU REALLY POST THAT ON YOUR PROFILE!?

ask about me.oh yea and i don't drive so if thats a problem then move on from my profile.well if you are still here and like what you read hit me up.also i'm good for conversations.i don't expect much from this site just to talk to people.
First Date:
up for anything

Blogger Commentary:

Hey, Keanu Reeves (from the Matrix) called and wants his "look" back! He doesn't drive huh? Probably a by-product of his drinking at least 3 times a week! He's looking for a "nice woman that don't care" - you gotta love a guy who sets the bar low. Anything over that mark is just a bonus to him!

Hit Me Up With Yo Money!!

Headline: **if u not talking abt muney dnt hmu**

About Me: Most of da time iam working iam busy person i listen music wen iam abt go bed iam funny person i lik make people laugh

First Date:

Iam cool gt along wit jst dnt cme at me wrng i lik shop go out to eat movies ihve one daughter she mean the world to me iam single parent about go back school for earlychild hood edu. anything else u ned kno jst hmu

Blogger Commentary:

Again here we go with the god-awful incomprehensible ghetto-speak! Her profile says she has some college.

DID YOU REALLY POST THAT ON YOUR PROFILE!?

Seriously where are these people going to college? McUniversity? Pulling their college courses off the dollar menu? Holy crap this country is so Effed, if these are our future leaders! Anyway, I digress.
Ok fellas' you may want to bring the GHB (date rape drug) and use it on yourself to get through a night with this one!

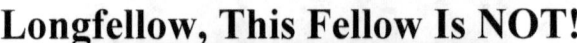

Longfellow, This Fellow Is NOT!

About Me:
Who am I? I'm independence, gallant, truth, vigor, loyalty, I'm a strong man only because a strong women has instilled that ability, I HAVE MY OWN EVERYTHING which makes me an asset not a liability. Who am I ??????
Well, they call me Brother to the night. And right now I'm

the blues in your left thigh... trying to become the funk in your right. Is that all right? I'm mental stimulation...I love long walks through an intriguing mind that I can adorn with appreaction. Where some say love is dead because they hung it with a rope. I say Im faith because a soul is lost without hope. Who am I? I'm a survivor carrying chivalry on my back, through the wire ive become a man just waitin for the right woman who can appreciate that. Is that alriiiight? *WHO ARE U???*** Well...if u got this far then u know my name is [REMOVED]. Yes a lil love [REMOVED] and a lot of me combined
Are there any women who love cooking anymore?
*** My ideal woman should have these qualities...loyalty,honesty,spontaneity,confidence,ambition ,self-sufficient,humor, patience, adventurous, creatively competitive ;-), enjoys being happy a lot more then being depressed..lol, and one who doesn't mind dressing up on special occasions ;-), one who loves movies with late nights and candle lights.

Blogger Commentary:

This guy attempts to wax poetic, and achieves an epic fail! He makes no point, we still know very little about him- other than he has a very healthy self-esteem!

DID YOU REALLY POST THAT ON YOUR PROFILE!?

Apparently Gangsta Poker Face Is Still Considered Attractive

Screen Name: **[REMOVED]**
Headline: **Words dnt mean nuthin only Action does !**
About Me:
I love to shop go to the movies,dinner,bowlin,I love to skate im very gd at it dnt test my skillz lol anyway I love to travel I love amusement parks and beaches I like to go to the casino penny machine only not much of a gambler Im very romantic easy to get along with I also have a low tolerence for bullshit,drama,games ect I am very blunt,striaght forward and I keep it a trillion so hmu ! :)
First Date:

A romantic dinner candle lite si on sum nice wine listen to m slow jamz then have alittle desert and talk and laugh and enjoy each other :D

Blogger Commentary:

Again, here we have more women who couldn't construct a legible sentence even if it meant getting a winning spot on their favorite lame-O reality TV show! They are still apparently under the delusion that absolute illiteracy and ghetto-speak is a desired trait to be passed down to their unfortunate offspring.

I like to also suppose that these are the same people who love to pull the "race" card when things don't go their way- "It's because I'm [INSERT ETHNICITY] Isn't it?" No sweetie, it's because you're dumb as hell, and you're obviously proud of it!
With this woman, only like-minded gangsta' types need apply, everyone else need not insult their intelligence, and steer clear!

DID YOU REALLY POST THAT ON YOUR PROFILE!?

.....Wow An Honest Man On A Dating Site?.....

Headline: **Discreet Good Times**

About Me:

To be totally honest with you..I am looking for ongoing discreet fun with a sexy partner. I want someone with a dirty mind & uninhibited drive.

I love to please. Nothing makes me happier than seeing you with a smile on your face & you feeling wonderful. I am a very giving person. What turns me on is turning you on...whatever it takes.

I am a great looking guy that is just missing some spice in his life. I have fantasies that have been left unfulfilled and would love to help you live out some of your dreams as well.

I have pictures I will gladly share with the right woman. Feel free to contact me & lets get a spectacular relationship started.

Feel free to add on the book, [REMOVED]

First Date:

146

As long as we are both smiling at the end...our date is successful.

-

Blogger Commentary:

Well this guy and the girl on the blog below him should totally hook up! They're looking for exactly the same thing-go figure! lol.

.....Well At Least She's Honest......

Headline: **looking for casual sexual encounters**
About Me:
Love to hang out.....like casual relationships and no strings attached....just having fun.....enjoy life...like abs on sexy

men.....interested in trying different
things....adventurous...thrill seeker/risk taker
First Date:
Watching sunset, romantic dinner, scary movie, then some
mind blowing break-your-back, you-my-b***h kind of sex

Blogger Commentary:

*At least this one is honest about what she is looking for! I
give her tons of credit for just putting it out there!*

I'm Too Sexy for A Photo
(At Least That's What He Keeps Telling Himself)

Headline: **Fools "Chase" B¡tches, Men "Wait" for
opportunity**
About Me:
yes I do have a real pictuie of me but it's not being shown
as I don't want my inbox blowing up, nor do I want to be
talked to because of looks... lame*
[Note:] but don't take me for a pushover, because I do not
have a picture up for I am Prince Fukin charming* lol
Descriptions suck..
To meet me or chat with me in person is the best way to
get to who I am because you cant get to know someone by
simply just reading about them.
If you believe that you can simply find a match by lazily
sittin on ya Phat ass, (P.H.A.T) pretty hot and temptingn;
rather then being in the field then you just simply retarded.

Daniel J Muhlestein

I'm just keepin it real and some of you aint gone like it.
PS. I like to joke a lot so you can't take me too seriously to
the heart.
[Note:] but take me serious when I say this though, there
are some intelligent women on here. About 60 percent are
intelligent, the rest of you B¡tchez need to swallow a case
of makeup so you can be pretty on the inside.
First Date:
50/50 Right down the middle.
K.i.s.s. theory, (keep it simple stupid.)
Dont be sloppy with ya mannerisms, fresh breath, always
be smellin good, clean clothes, if your wearing a dress no
granny panties please.
and if you like to get *uCked up from drinking I have no
time for you.
What a waste of time...
especially if you're Racist. If your " Racist " Fuk you all
together.
other than that if you made it this far cutie insert something
in my Inbox.

Blogger Commentary:

*I don't think I need to explain much about this guy. He
pretty much hangs himself! He thinks he is so "all that"
that he doesn't put a photo of himself on the page. He
speaks of women who have sloppy mannerisms, yet he can
barely handle the English language.*

DID YOU REALLY POST THAT ON YOUR PROFILE!?

I'm thinking this guy is going to be single for a while, that is, unless he hooks up with some of the women on this blog! Perhaps I should be a matchmaker!

Got A Little Gangsta In Me!

Headline: **what up motha ****a?!**

.......Swoon....She had me at "motha ****a?!"

About Me:

hey!! my hobbies are... drinkin with my best friend!! n gettin loud!! i like fishin, n bein outside... that covers all bases... :) i am goin to school n i work. im a tough girl not a lil **** so vagina boys n lard asses stay away!! i am down to try new things n go on new adventures... but not with mexicans... or black ppl... perty much if u aint white dont msg me... i dont like perty boys, i like rough n dirty... i dont like ur fancy space cars n all ur money. i like real men. if i dont msg back its prolly cuz i aint interested n ur prolly borin me... sooo with all this said, dont msg me sayin what a **** i am... dont waste ur time... i will just laugh at you... thanks!!!

Blogger Commentary:

She says she has some university- this is obvious in the way she writes. But to her credit, at least she had the decency of editing herself with asterisks (and for that we thank you).

This one is a bit racist- but hey, we all have the flavors that we're into. So I ain't haten' (oh crap, I'm starting to sound like her).

So there you have it boys, this one's a real keeper! - It's a shame that she looks so good, but is dumb as hell!

Uhhhhhh....He Thinks He's Cool....

About Me:
Single, very fit and attractive looking for ladies who are sexy, funny, love to have fun. witty a plus but can make exceptions if your real cute ! maybe!!!
Im looking to meet interesting attractive ladies to go out with and have fun.

Blogger Commentary:

Wow ladies, this guy don't seem shallow at all. It seems he's really down to earth. And if you look "real cute" AKA - BANGIN' HOT-but happen to be dumb as hell, he may make an exception for you. What a gracious fellow, this guy!

Hooked On Phonics
Sure Worked For This One!

About Me:
hey im [REMOVED] im 21 im full mexican im cool easy
goin and im looking for a kool guy to talk to and get to
knw even dou i dnt think im ever gonna find wat im lookin
for in here but i nv knw im amayb pretty and thick and
sweet but i havent found ma guy i dnt got kids n i need a
serious man not someone to just talk to but also get ro
knwake him mine n if ur talkin to me its only me not the
whole [REMOVED] site cuz i got alot of homegurlss in
here that i knw n its not cute wen we find out we been
talkin to the same guy ! so get at me if ur serious if not
peace out,!

DID YOU REALLY POST THAT ON YOUR PROFILE!?

Blogger Commentary:

Now you have just gotta find it super sexy that not only does this girl have mad grammar skills, but that she is posing with the "duck lips" with her fingers cocked like a gun! Oh baby!!

And what's with this speak of all her "homegurlss?" Home Girls (for us literate types). Am I gonna get jumped if I date this one? -Doesn't she just make you feel all warm, safe and cuddly inside?

I think I may want to bring her to Easter dinner to meet my mom and family!

Gee I Didn't Know Paris Hilton Was Available!

About Me
-Music
-Beach
-Candy
-Boys With Tattoos
-Money
-Cars
-Shopping
-Being adored
-Spoiled
Just need one to prove there not all the same...
I'm not the how type you spit game to I'm the wifey type
you give your last name to...

Blogger Commentary:

*Wow, this one seems like the type to get engrossed in deep
meaningful conversation- about Prada, Gucci, and Louis*

DID YOU REALLY POST THAT ON YOUR PROFILE!?

Vuitton. More apt to ask for your credit card before wanting to meet your kids. If you're riding in a car worth less than eighty grand, she wouldn't be seen is such a beater! And if you're not showering her with gifts and singing her praises 24-7, she just may move on to a more qualified suitor.

So there ya have it fellas! -If you're into plastic in all its various forms, this one's for you!

My Doppelgänger Is a Muppet? I Need A Redo!

Blogger Commentary:

It's never a good sign when someone sees your photo and the first thing that comes to mind is that you look like a

Muppet. You probably should have thought your "high fashion" through a bit more thoroughly.

But then again, maybe she's looking for the Fozzie Bear type- which may be her perfect match! Ya just never know now do ya!

DID YOU REALLY POST THAT ON YOUR PROFILE!?

Strictly Dickly- WTF?

About Me:
First off Imma start by saying, If your gonna message me and b creepy, or just want sex. Please save us both the time and effort and just don't message me. I can have sex w/ enough guys if I wanted to, I'm looking for a guy that will like me for who I am. I understand Chivalry is dead but Dam.. Anyways I'm new to [REMOVED], been here for a few months. I like to pretty much just Hang out with my friends and party a little bit. I'm easily entertained, so the first time we meet don't put to much thought into it. To save us both the trouble and awkwardness of me telling you in person, I am Transgendered. Love it or Hate it, I've

accepted it and hopefully I can find a guy who will do the same. If you have any other questions just ask (:

Blogger Commentary:

First of all- any guy who sees a mouth surrounded by spikes- should quickly run away! -looks more like a trap than a mouth!

....And as we hear the screeching halt of the record player...   DID "SHE" JUST SAY TRANSGENDERED!?   YIKES!

Hi:) I Get Paid On The 3rd Of Each Month!

Age: 20
Education: Some College
Profession: Artist
About Me:
im a kool grl 2 chill with..I likk 2 have fun...I dnt take no
bull frm nobdy..crack jokes maken pple laugh..Im a artist I
do tattoos sumtymes an I do alil graffiti an traveling an
shopping...My type of music is rapp,pop,r&b

Blogger Commentary:

*What the hell is up with this grammar? Is this what our
colleges are teaching these days? No wonder America is*

*behind the curve compared to the rest of the world- its
people who spell like this!*

*So she's a professional artist? AKA Prison Tattoos. -And
graffiti? Last I checked that's illegal. So really she's saying
she's broke as a joke!*
Sounds like a real winner, this one!

Trying To Figure Out Exactly What's She Got?

The following is this girl's "points of interest" on her
dating profile:

I Got My Own

18 Yr. old.

Some college

Profession: Dancing,Doing my makeup

About Me:

- I'm very intelligent I'm not a real club going girl but if
I'm feeling myself I will go and im the oldest girl my mom
have I want to have something in life I don't like men that
talk to you next day they don't know you exist I'm sexy fun

DID YOU REALLY POST THAT ON YOUR PROFILE!?

talented I'm a real good kisser I love hanging out with he girls but I will make time for my man when we want me to and when I love I, I LOVE FORREAL ian on that fake sh*tand if you look at my pic and don't read what point of it inbox in me if you don't anything about me... Any More Questions??hmuu youu guys

First Date:

Our first date would have to be dinner a walk through a park or a museum or some and then we would just watch the sunset I guess and cuddle.... Etc(I don't **** on first dates)

Blogger Commentary:

Now OBVIOUSLY she is very intelligent as she states. Her command of the English language is astonishing! I wonder what she would be like during that museum tour she says she would like to go on for the first date. -Maybe she meant the Children's Museum?

Professional dancer and makeup "artist" -That's definately someone to take home to mamma!

*She says "I don't ****on first dates" - So the second date, she's ALL IN! NICE :)*

GOOD LUCK FELLAS!

More Lips Than Hips?......I'm Not Sure If I Wanna Know!

Oh......My.....Gosh......
(Shaking my head in disbelief)

Geee...I Wonder What Her IN Box Looks Like?

Hi! My name is [REMOVED]. I am 5'6" and weight 115 pounds. I love fitness and have devoted my time to this passion. I teach body pump/attack. I can set aside fitness and be a great partner. ;)

Blogger Commentary:

And that's all her description says! She is OBVIOUSLY looking for an honest upstanding man! OMG! LMAO!

Blow Up Doll

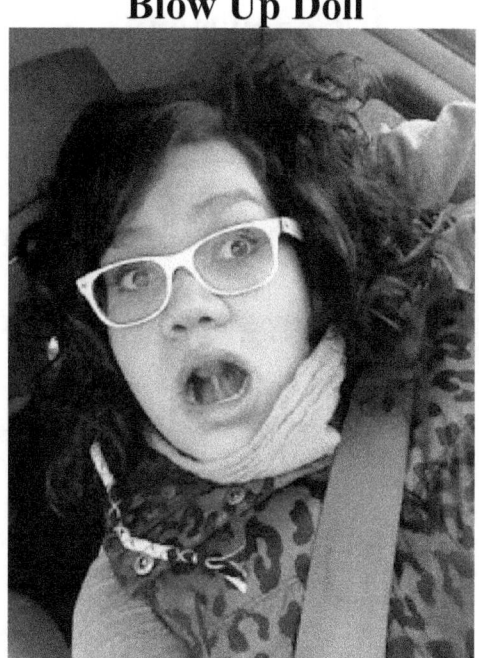

Blogger Commentary:

I think I shall dub this unfortunate photo BLOW UP DOLL! And this is her actual MAIN photo on the dating site! Good luck guys with this one!

Conclusion

Thank you for your time in reading about this very interesting journey I have gone through in the depths of Internet dating hell! My view of women and Internet dating has been forever changed. I have so much more respect for what women have to put up with on dating sites.

As of this writing, I am still single....

www.ingramcontent.com/pod-product-compliance
Lightning Source LLC
Chambersburg PA
CBHW051508170526
45166CB00001B/445